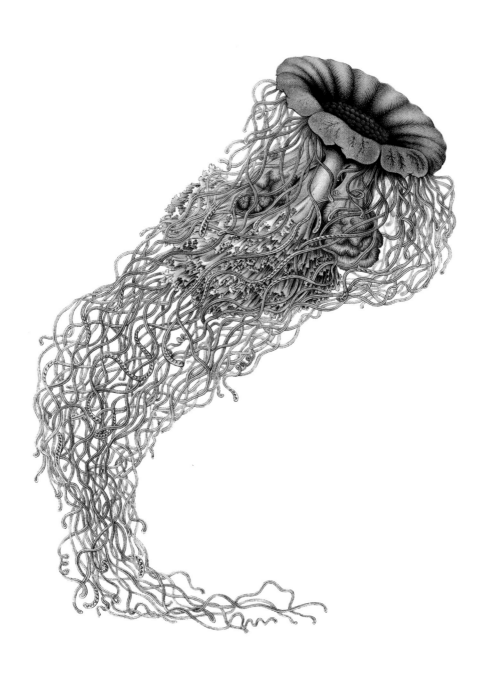

SEA LIFE

SEA LIFE

DOVERPICTURA

DOVER PUBLICATIONS, INC. | Mineola, New York

Selected and designed by Althea Chen, Amy Stein, and Alan Weller.

Sea Life is a new work, first published by Dover Publications, Inc., in 2006.

For permission to use more than ten images, please contact:
Permissions Department
Dover Publications, Inc.
31 East 2nd Street
Mineola, NY 11501
rights@doverpublications.com

The CD-ROM file names correspond to the images in the book. All of the artwork stored on the CD-ROM can be imported directly into a wide range of design and word-processing programs on either Windows or Macintosh platforms. No further installation is necessary.

International Standard Book Number: 0-486-99668-9

Manufactured in the United States of America
Dover Publications, Inc., 31 East 2nd Street, Mineola, NY 11501
www.doverpublications.com

004

005

006

007

008

009

9

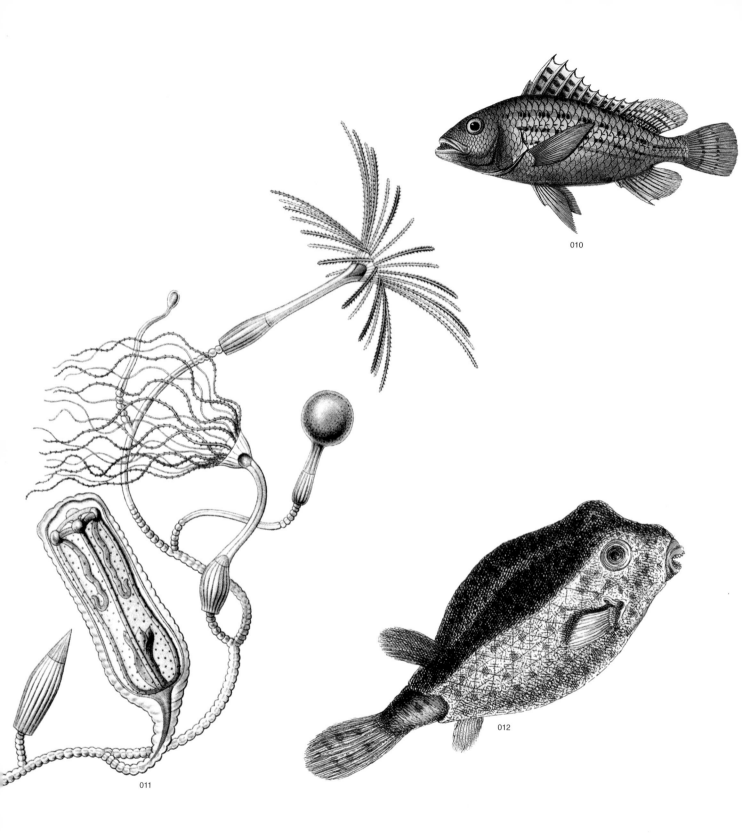

010

011

012

013

014

015

016

017

018

019

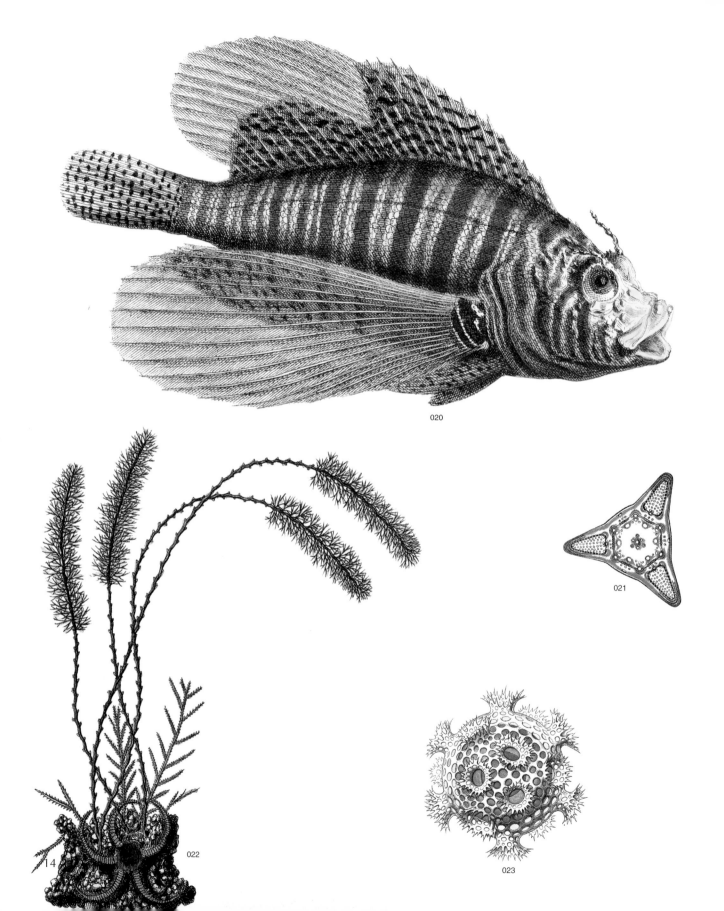

020

021

022

14

023

024

025

026

027

15

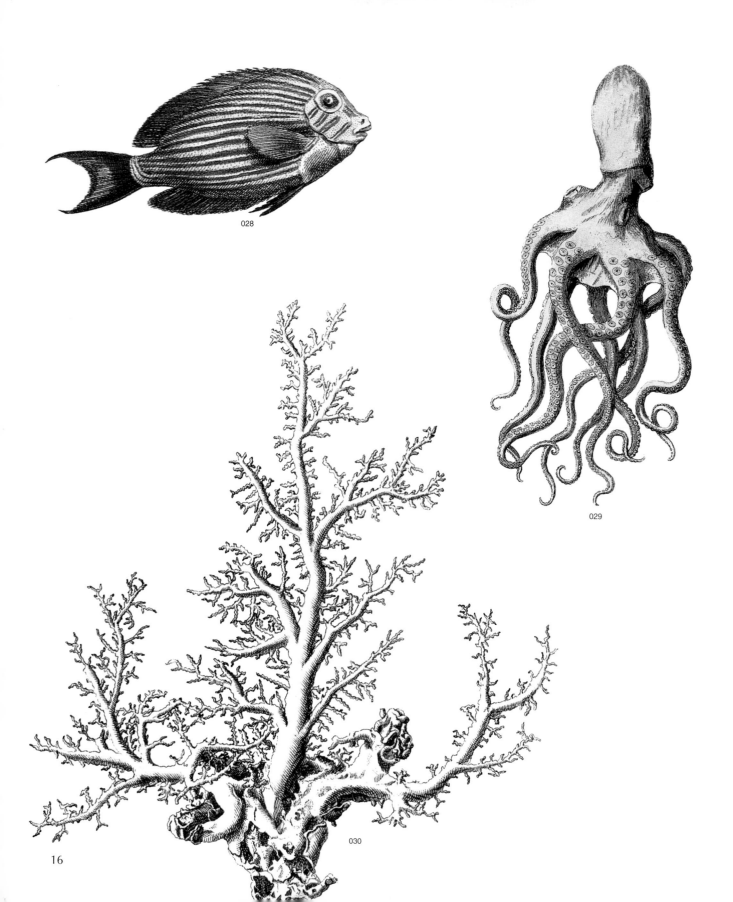

028

029

030

16

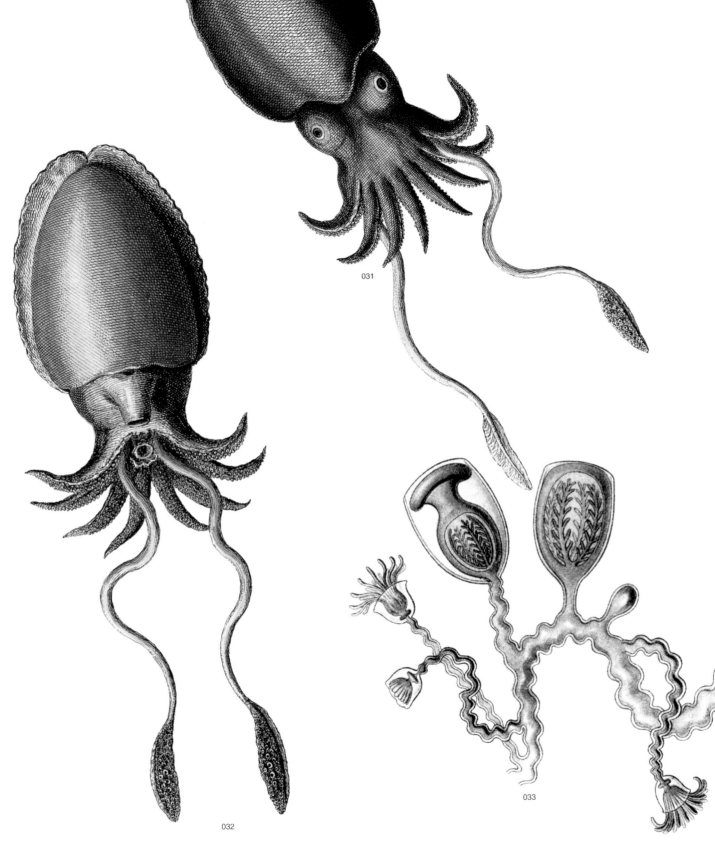

031

032

033

034

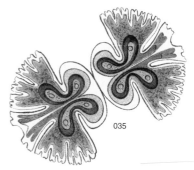

035

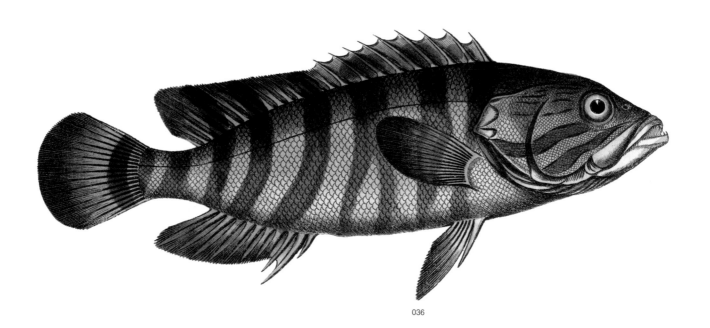

036

037

18

038

039

040

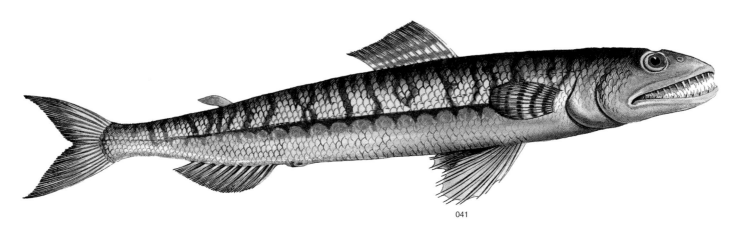

041

042

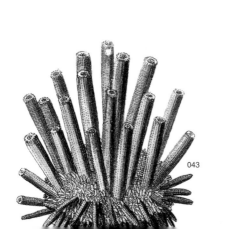

043

044

045

046

21

047

048

24

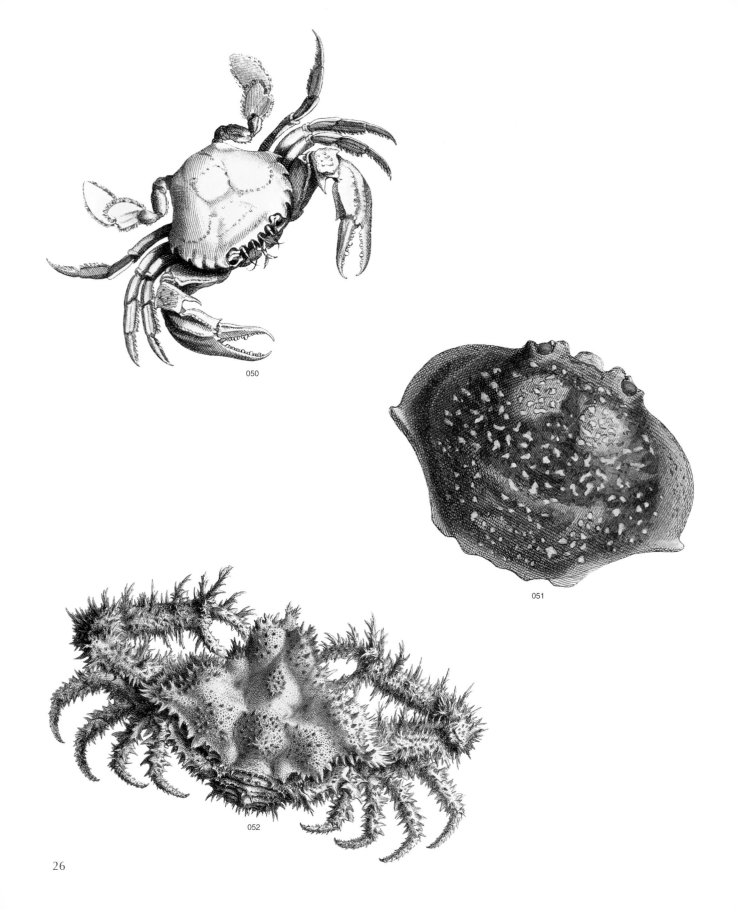

050

051

052

053

054

055

056

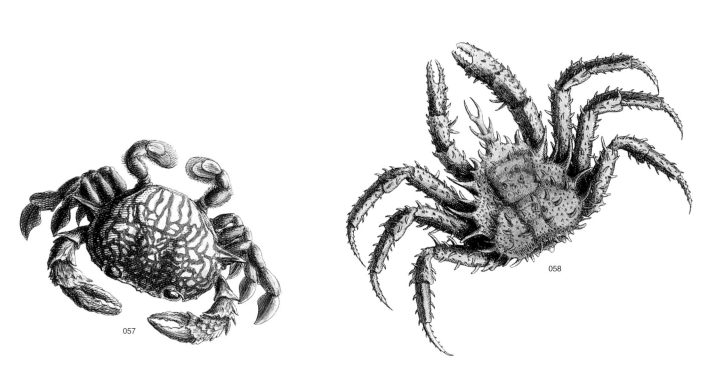

057

058

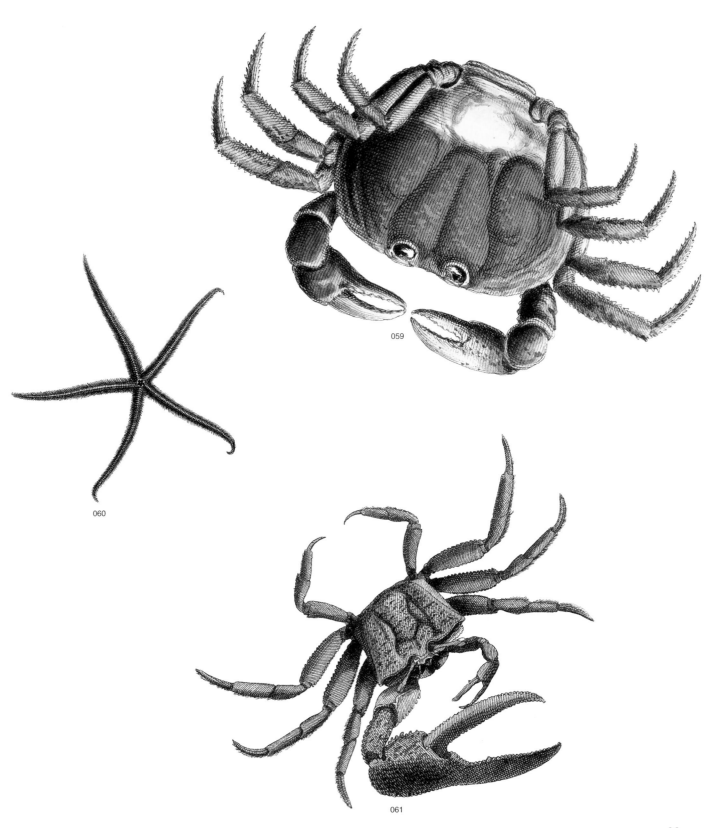

059

060

061

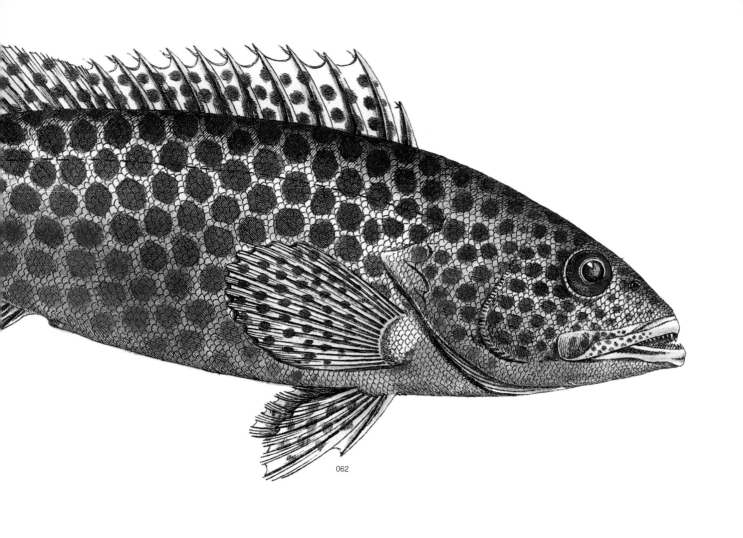

062

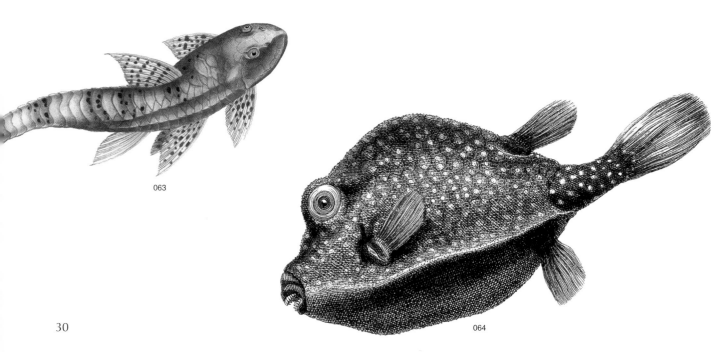

063

064

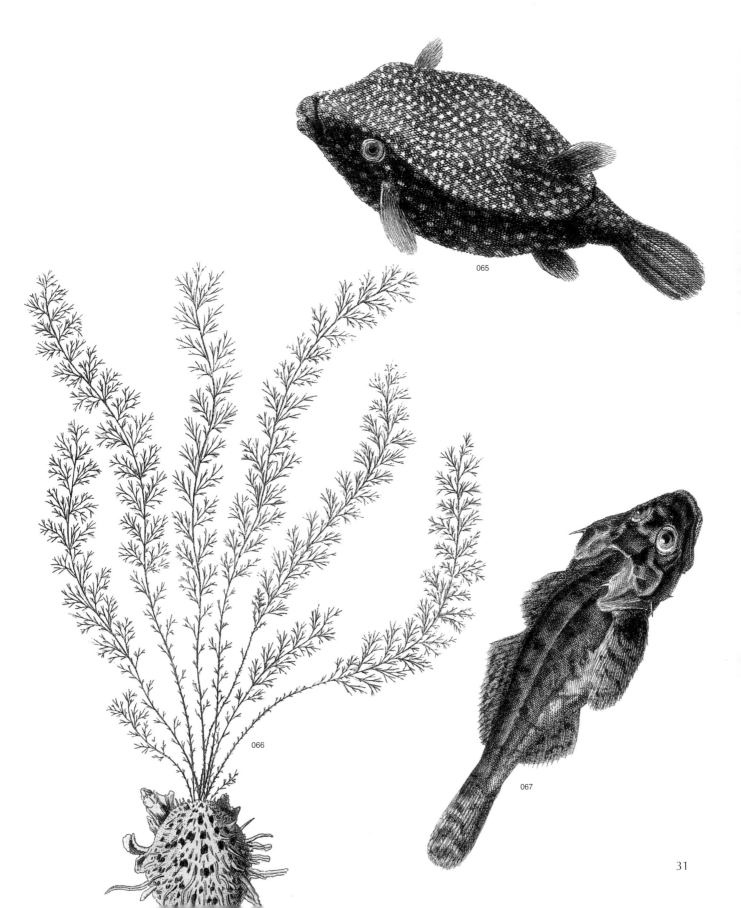

065

066

067

068

069

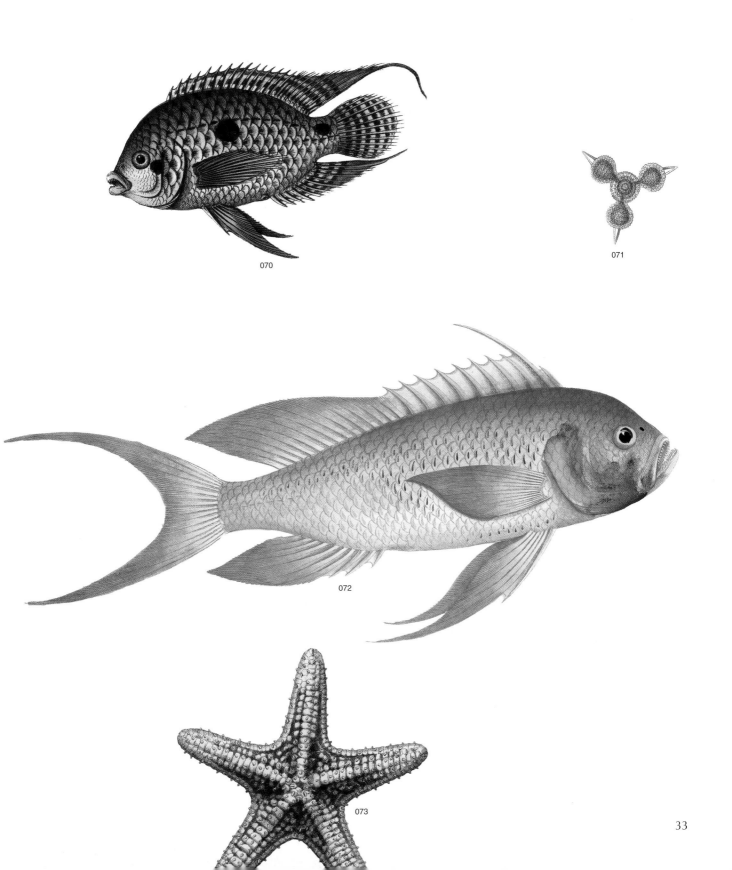

070

071

072

073

33

074

075

076

077

078

079

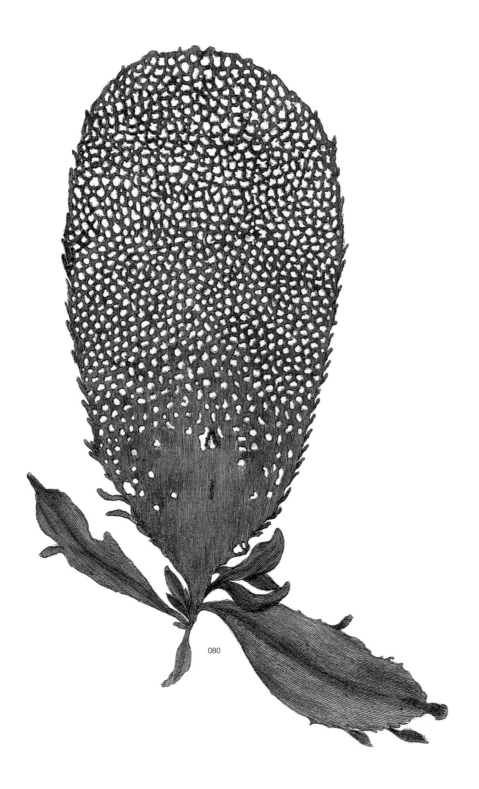

080

081

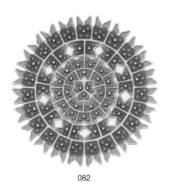

082

083

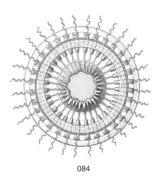

084

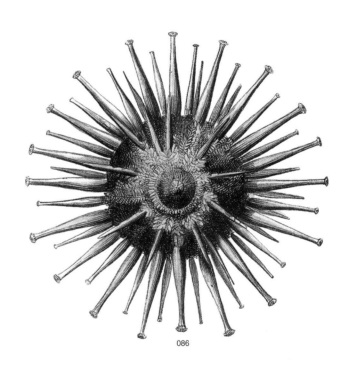

086

085

37

087

088

089

090

091

092

093

094

096

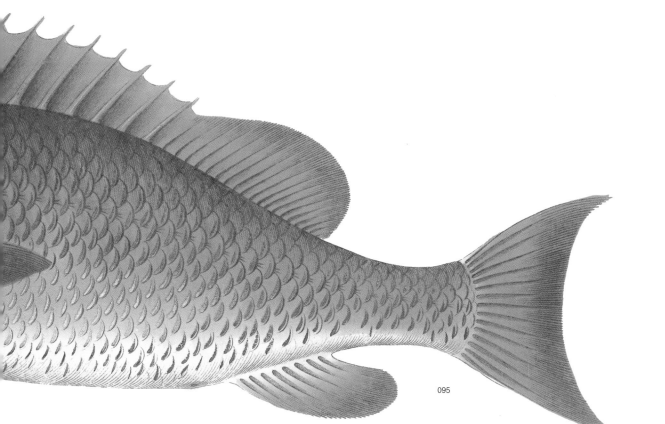

095

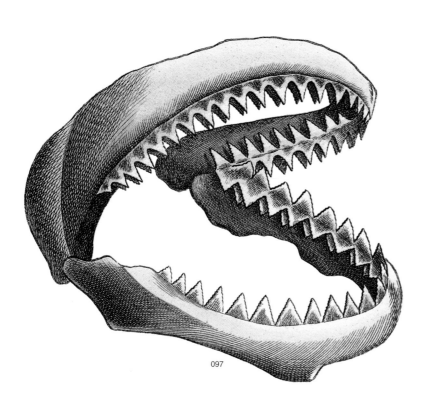

097

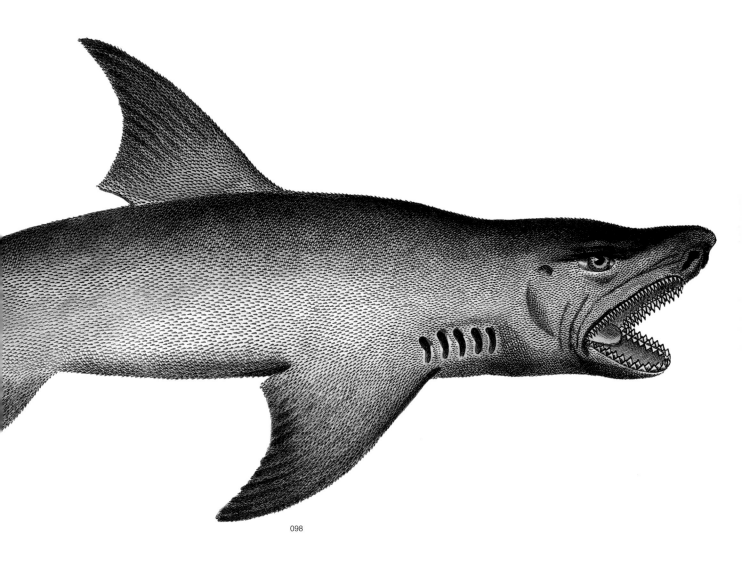

098

099

100

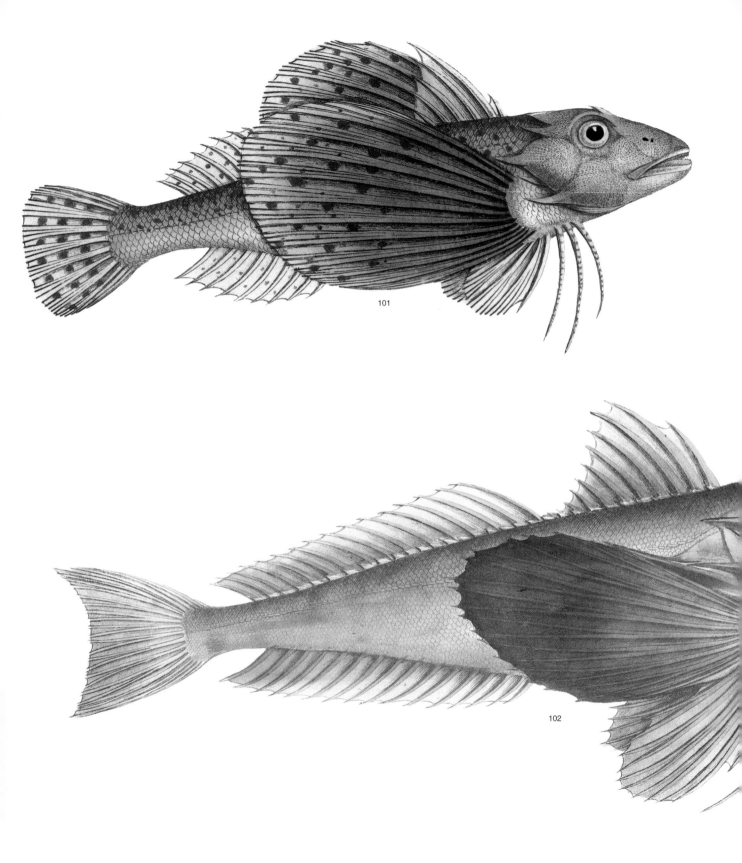

101

102

103

104

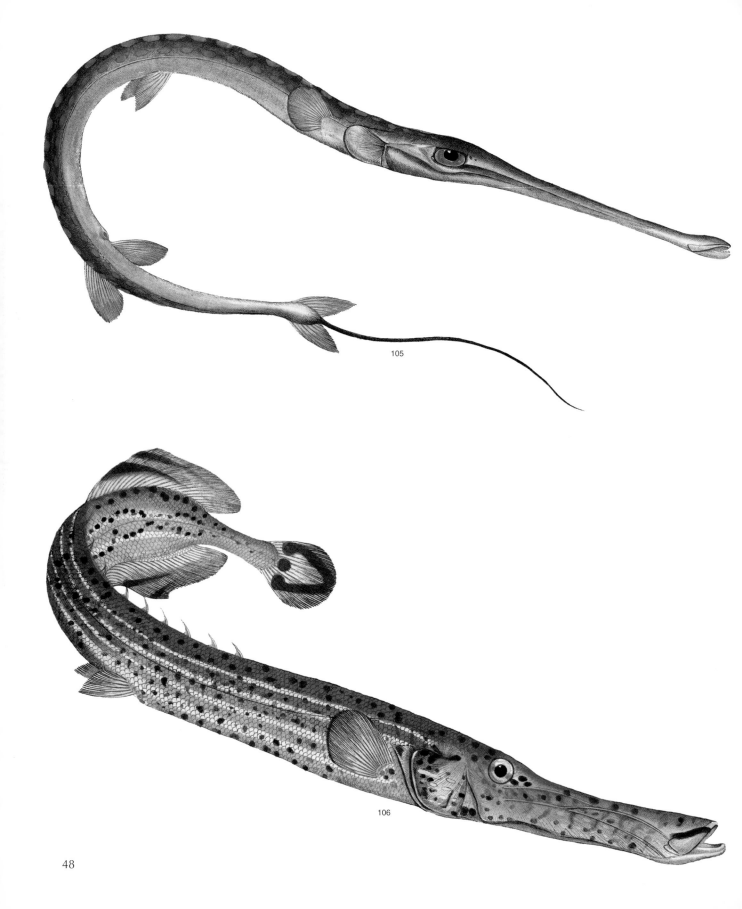

105

106

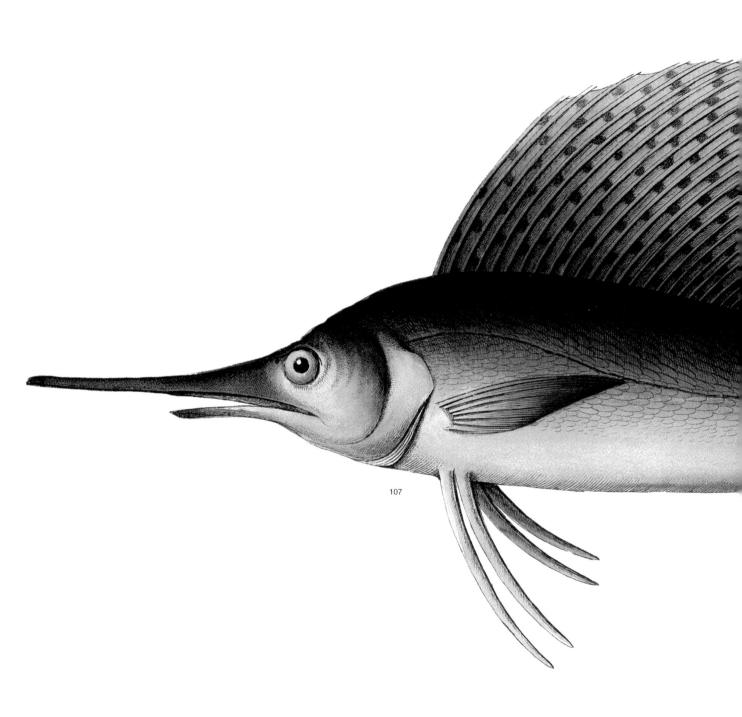

107

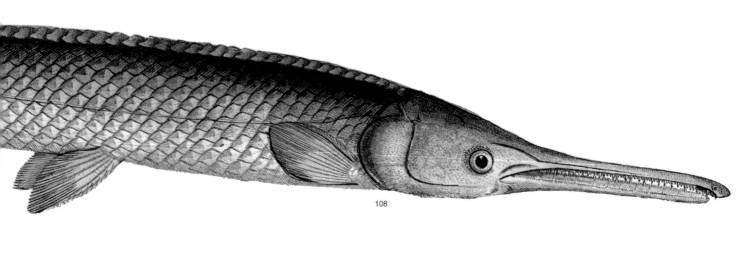

108

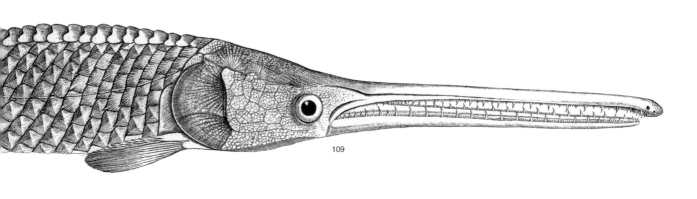

109

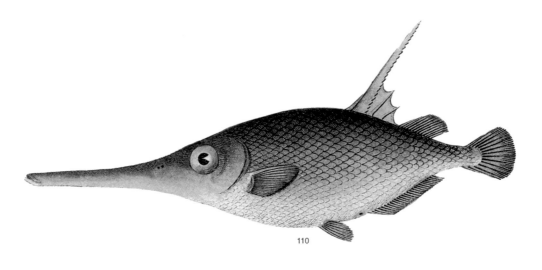

110

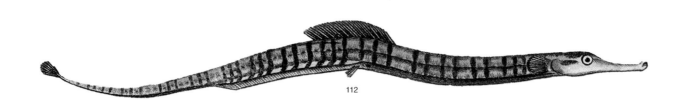

111

112

113

114

115

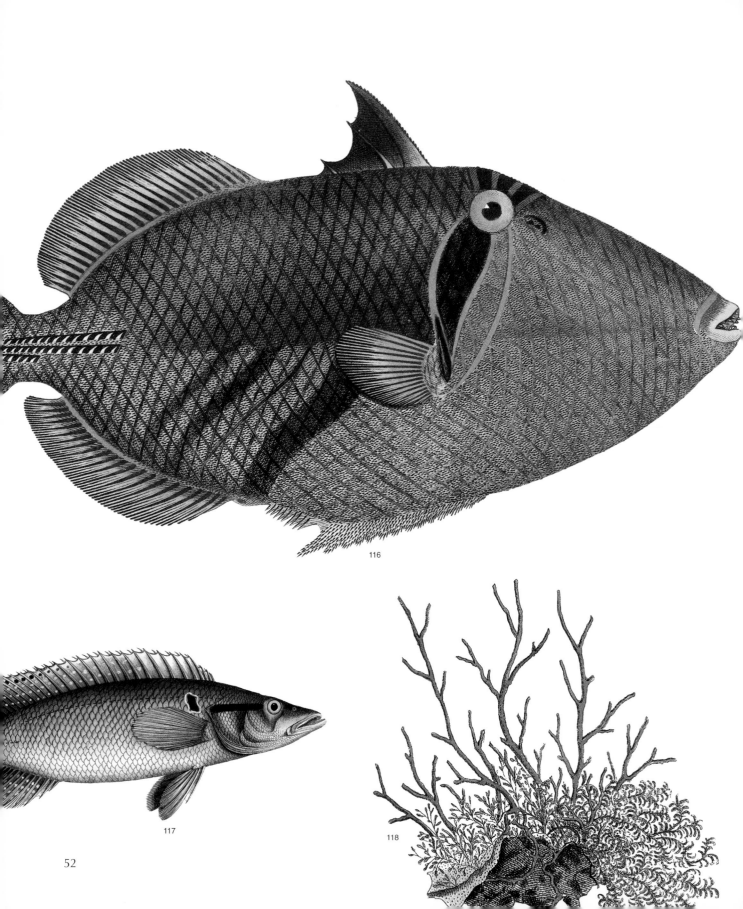

116

117

118

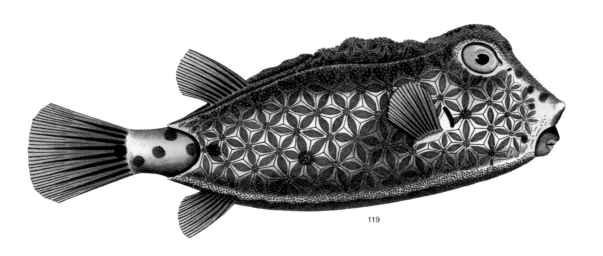

119

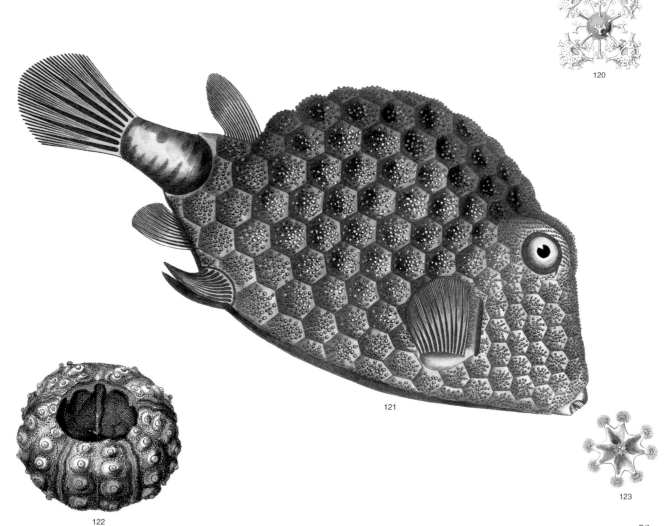

120

121

122

123

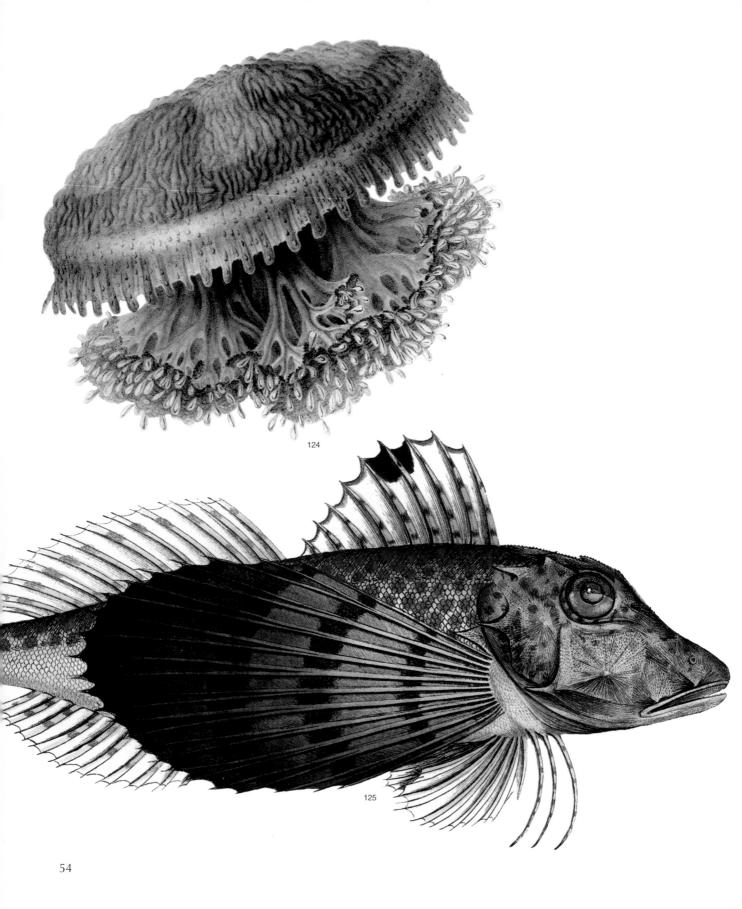

124

125

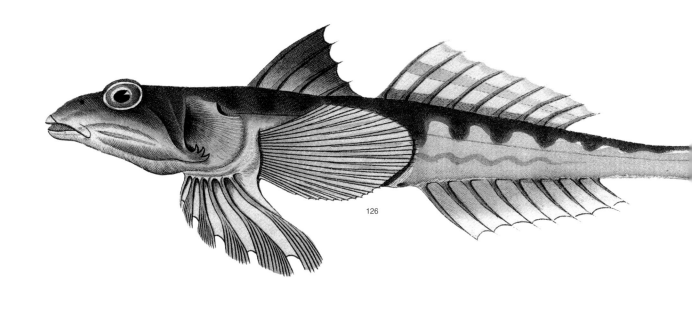

126

127

128

129

130

131

132

133

134

135

136

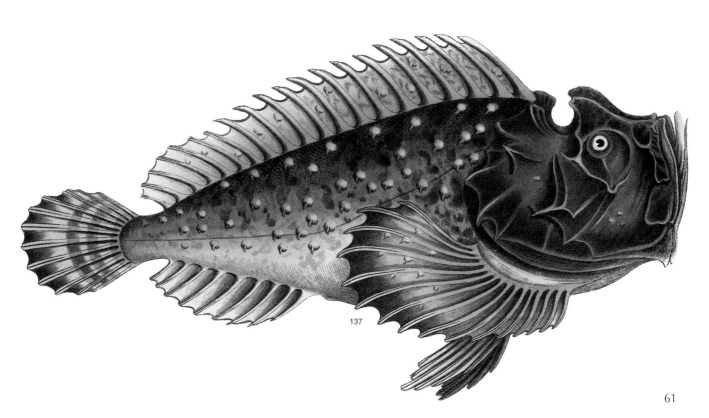

137

138

139

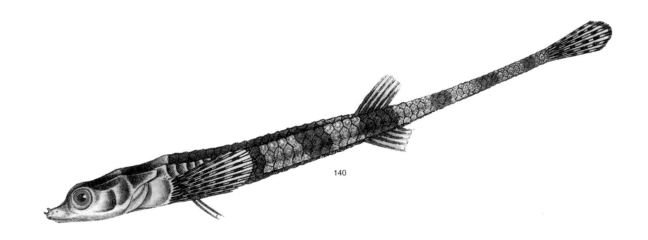

140

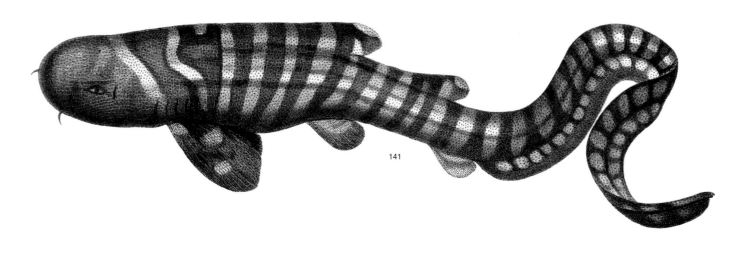

141

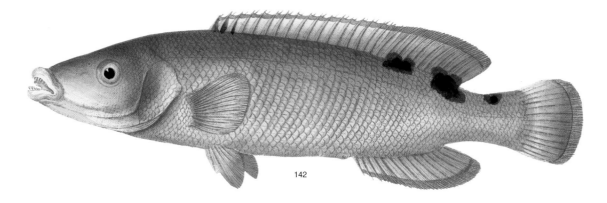

142

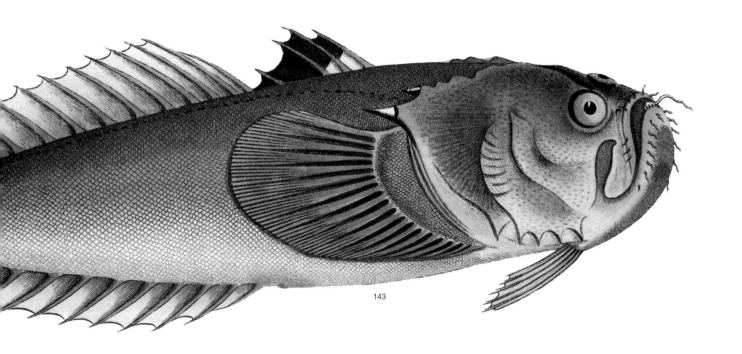

143

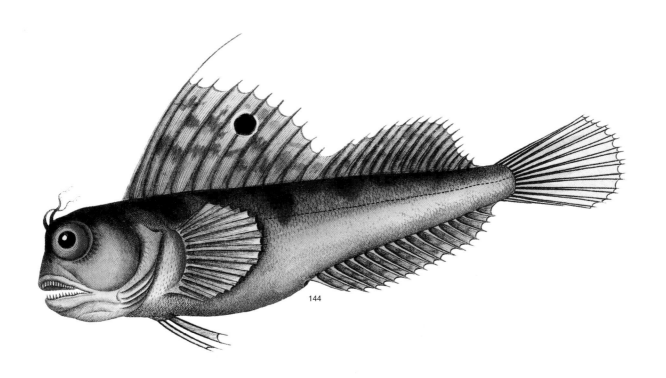

144

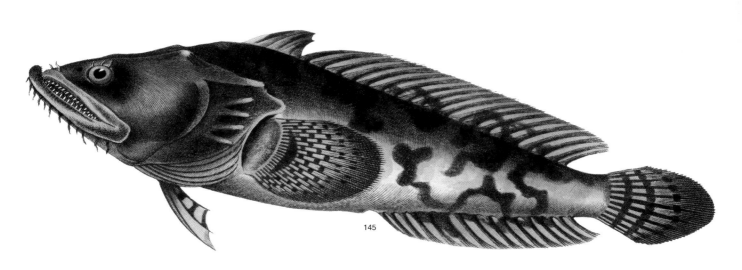

145

146

147

148

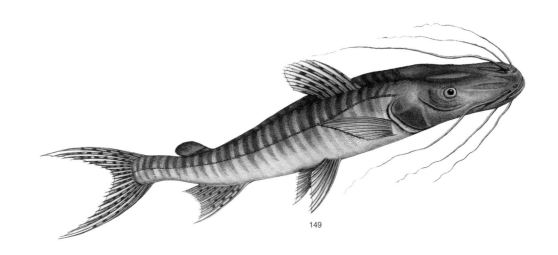

149

150

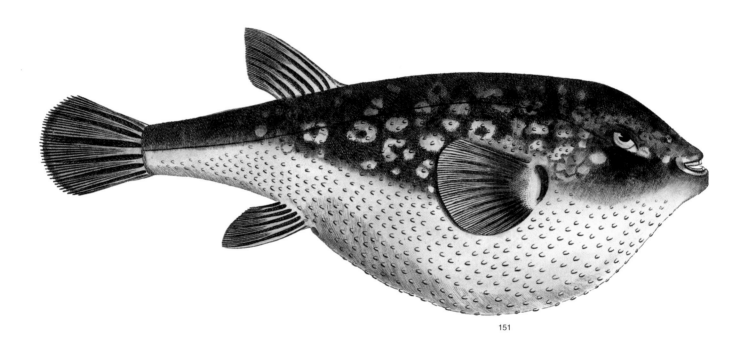

151

152

153

154

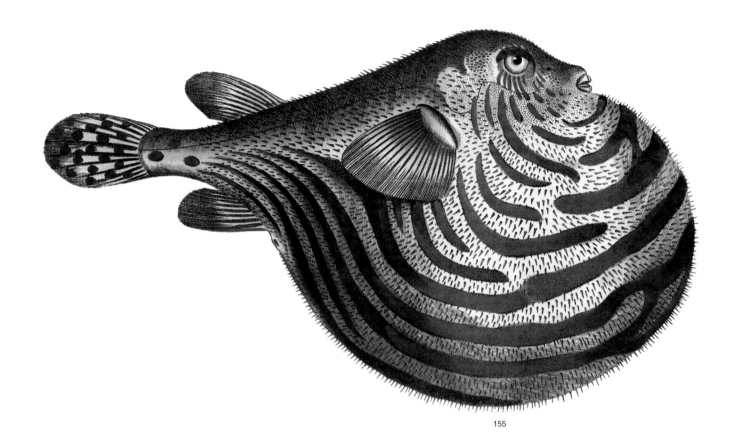

155

156

157

158

159

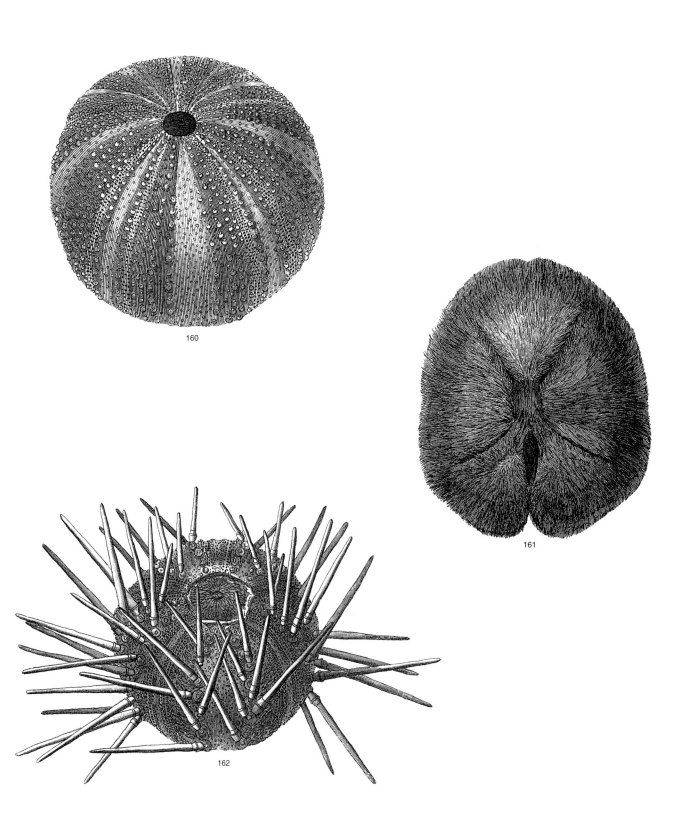

160

161

162

163

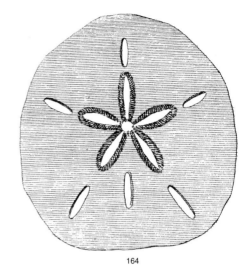

164

165

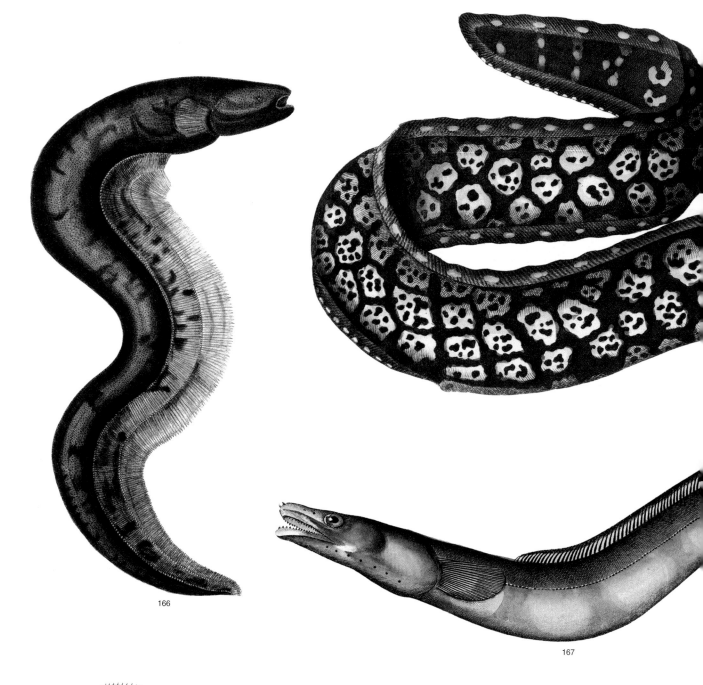

166

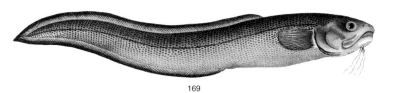

167

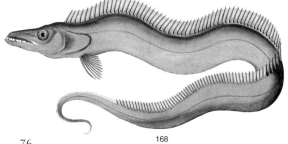

168

169

170

171

172

173

174

175

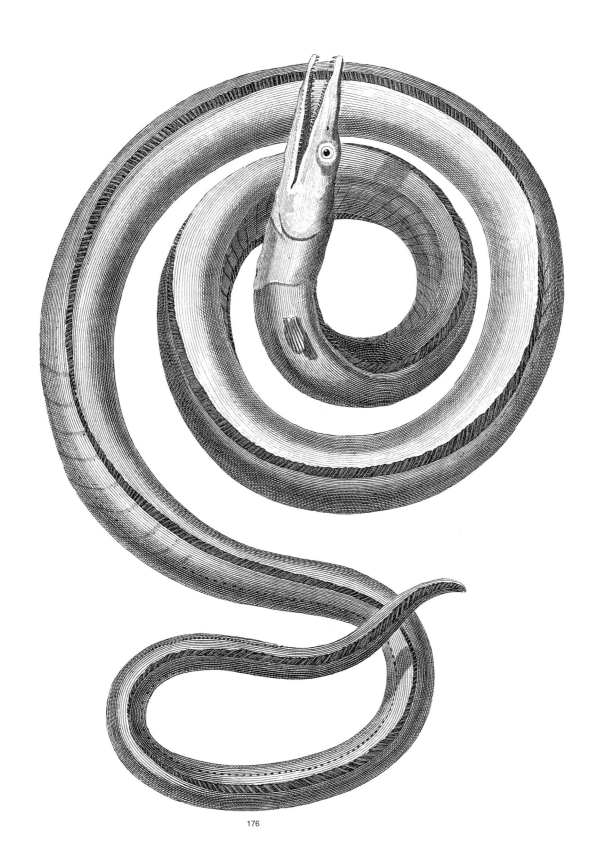

176

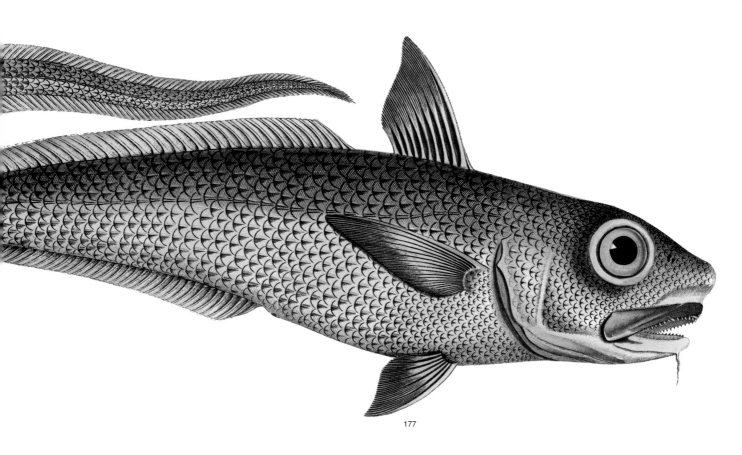

177

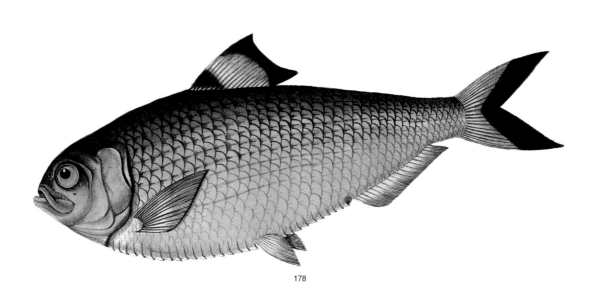

178

179

180

181

182

183

184

185

186

187

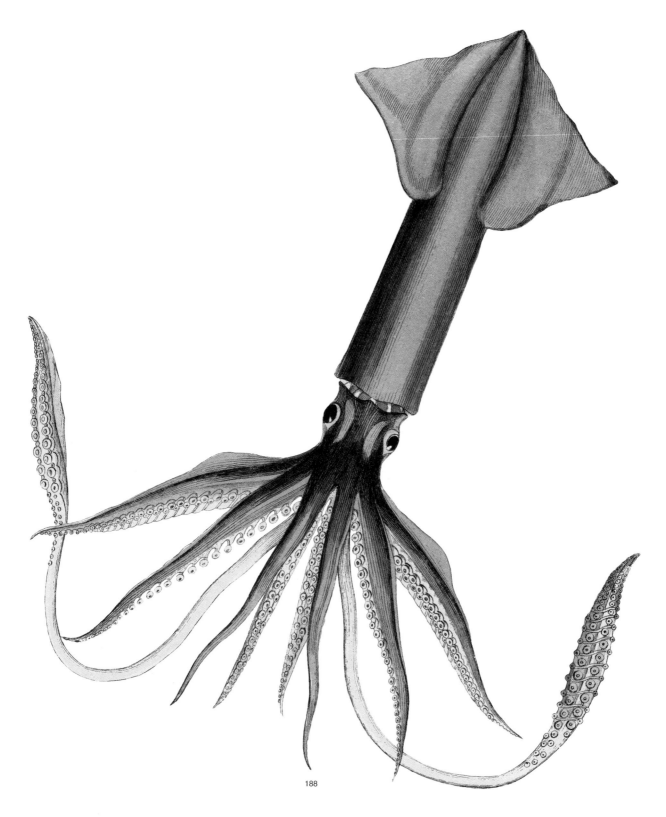

188

189

190

191

192

193

194

195

196

197

198

199

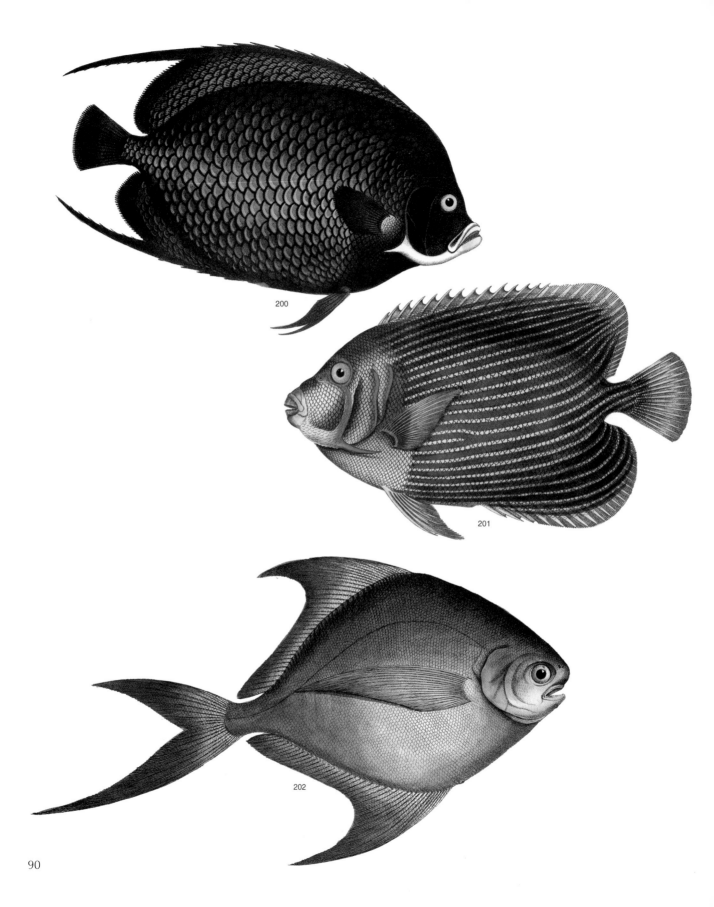

200

201

202

203

204

205

206

207

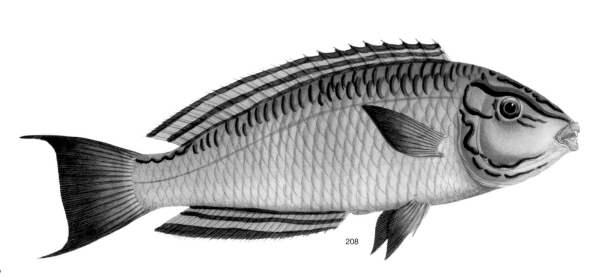

208

209

210

211

212

213

214

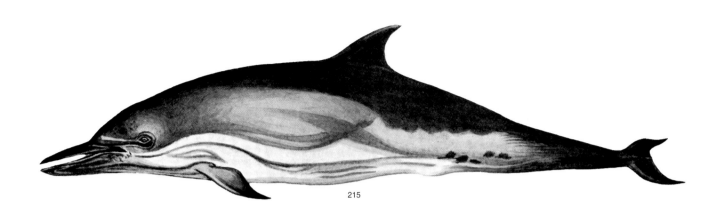

215

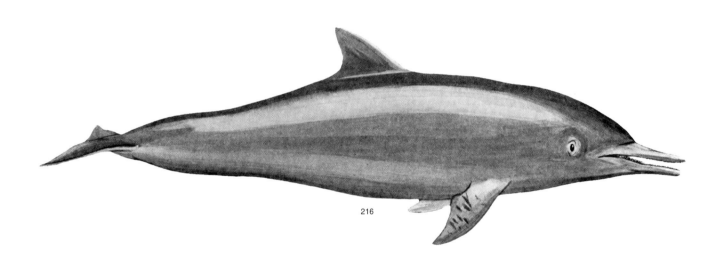

216

217

218

219

1.

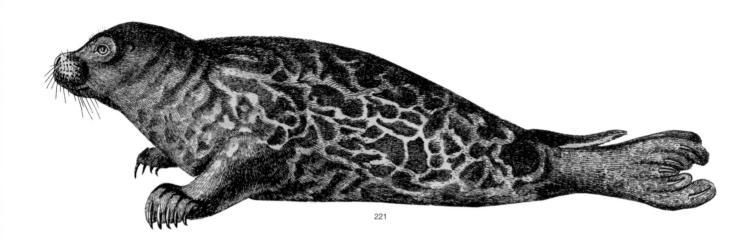

221

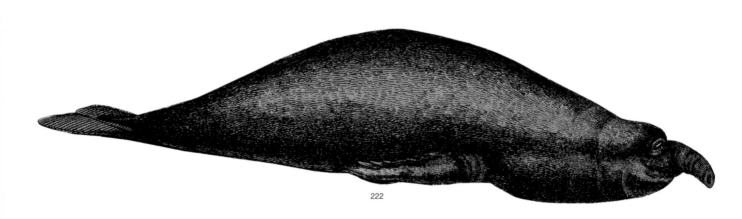

222

223

224

225

226

227

228

229

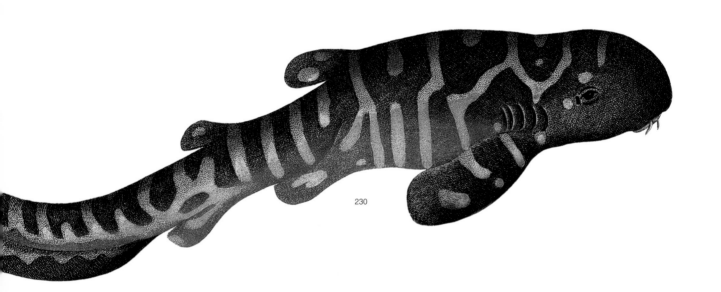

230

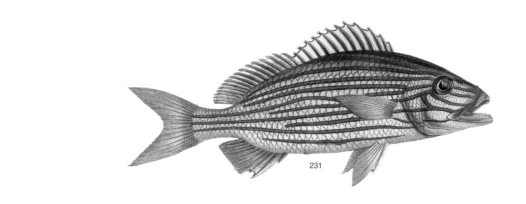

231

232

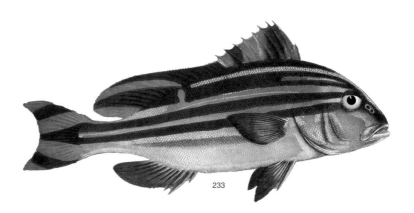

233

234

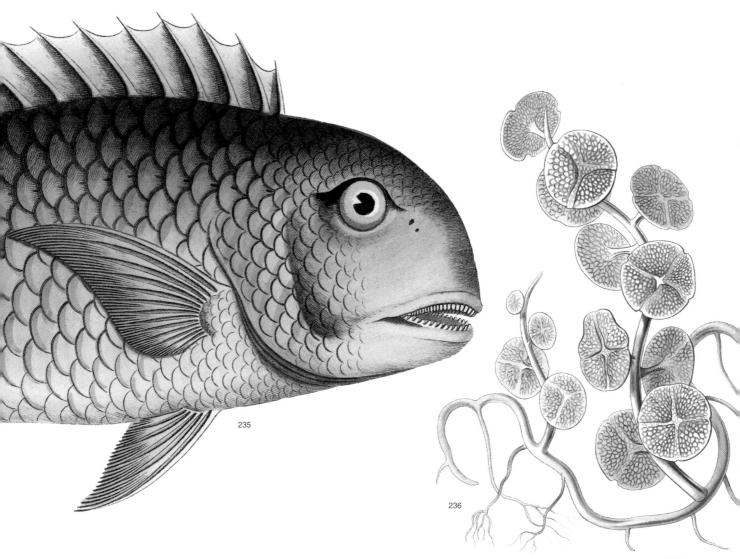

235

236

237

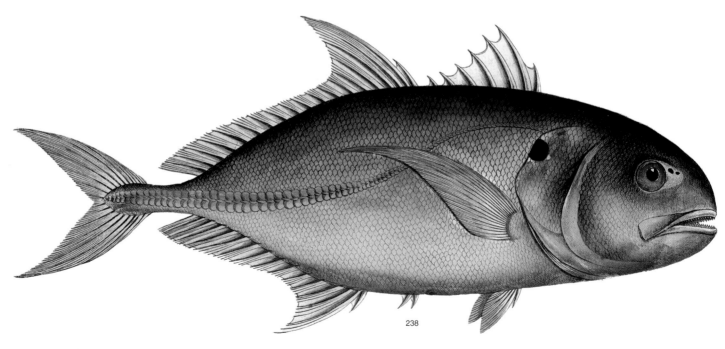

238

239

240

241

242

243

244

245

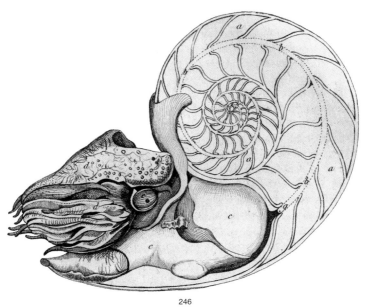

246

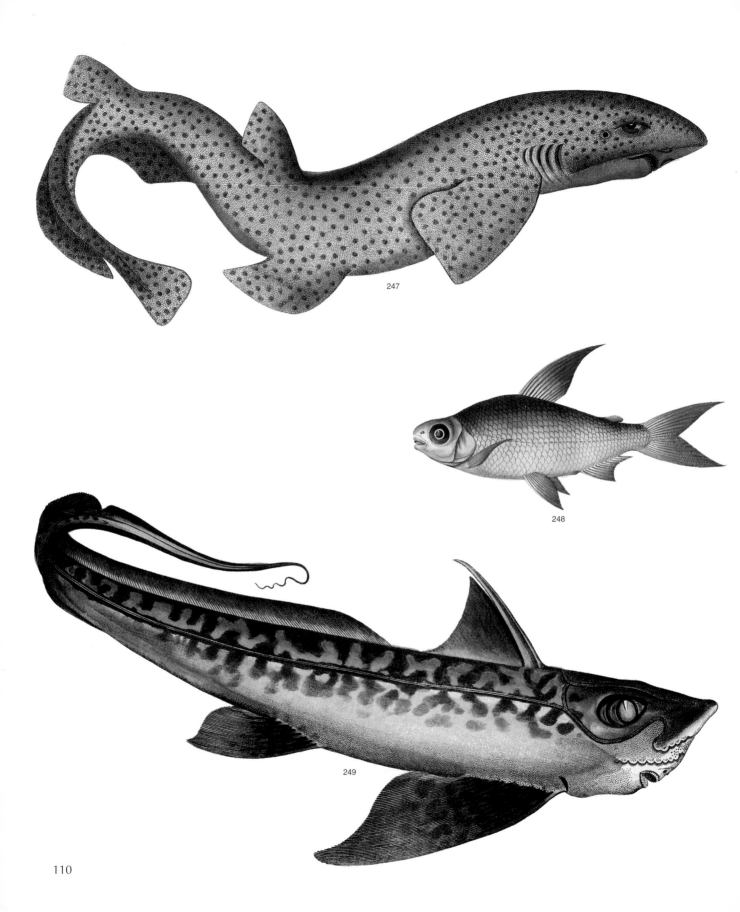

247

248

249

250

251

252

253

254

255

256

257

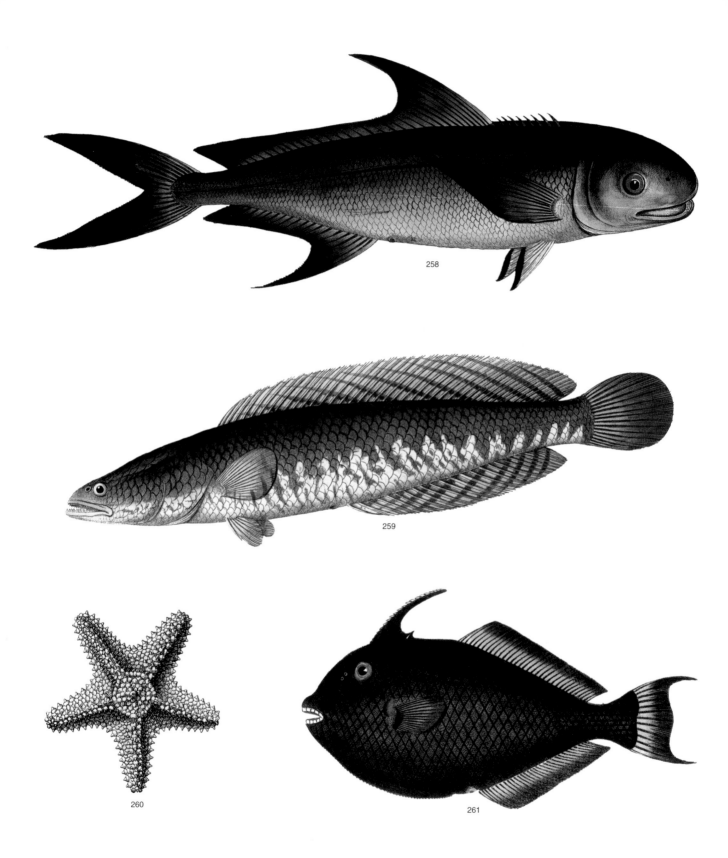

258

259

260

261

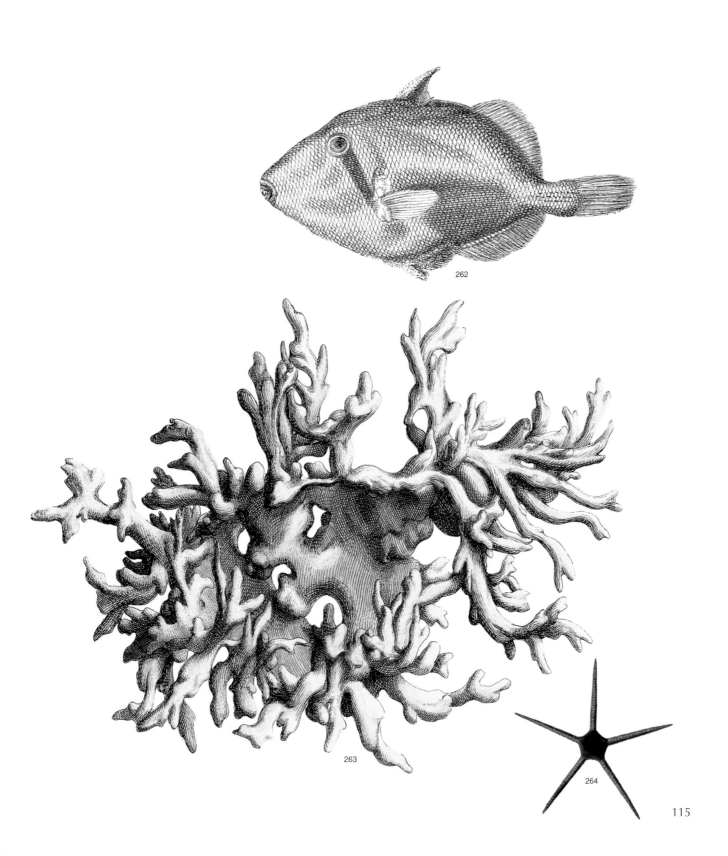

262

263

264

265

266

267

268

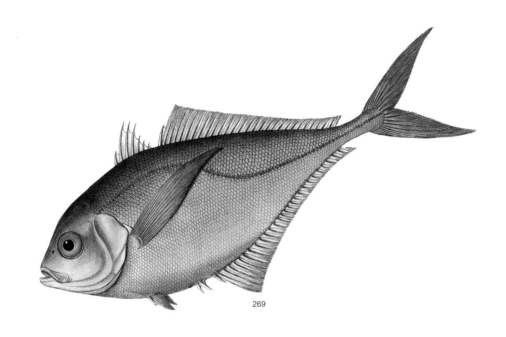

269

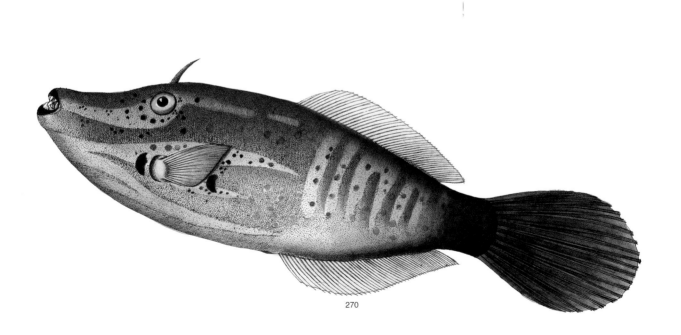

270

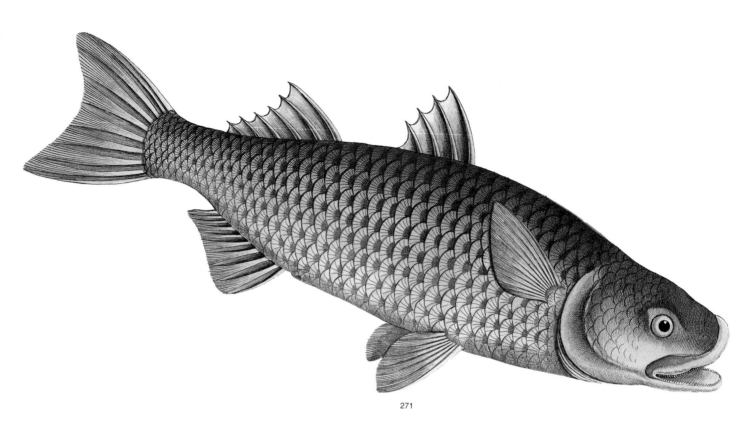

271

272

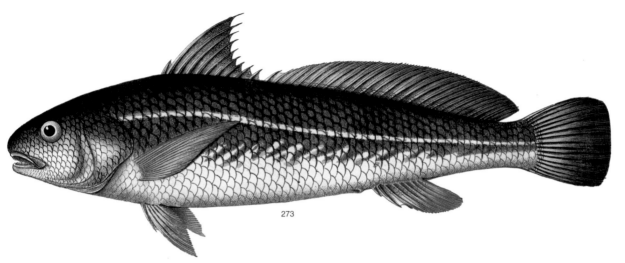

273

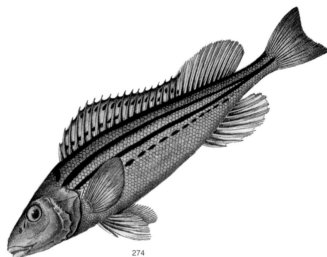

274

275

119

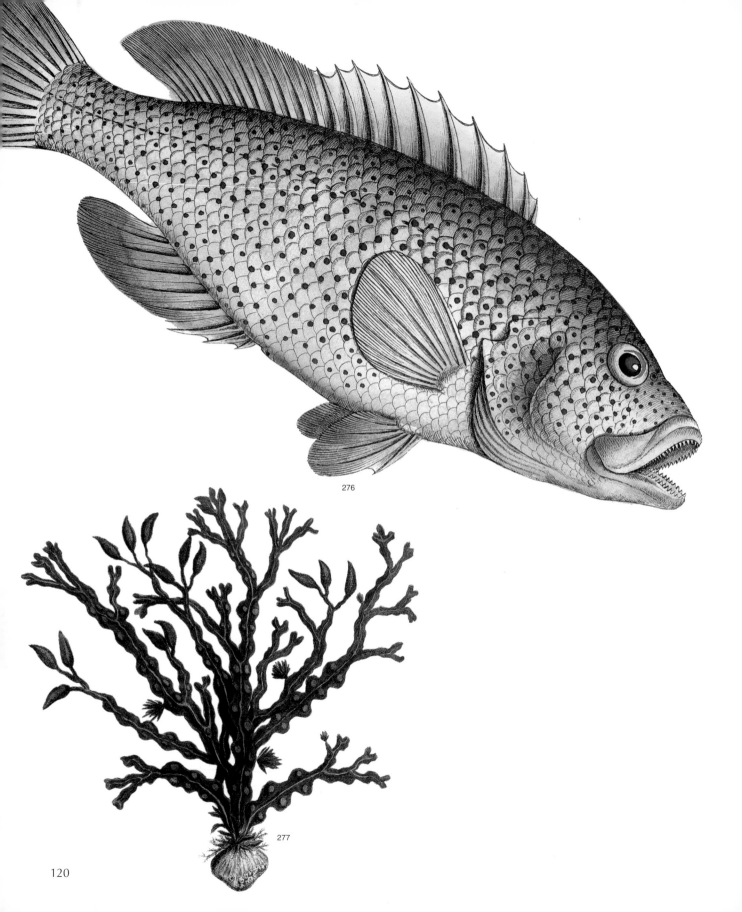

276

277

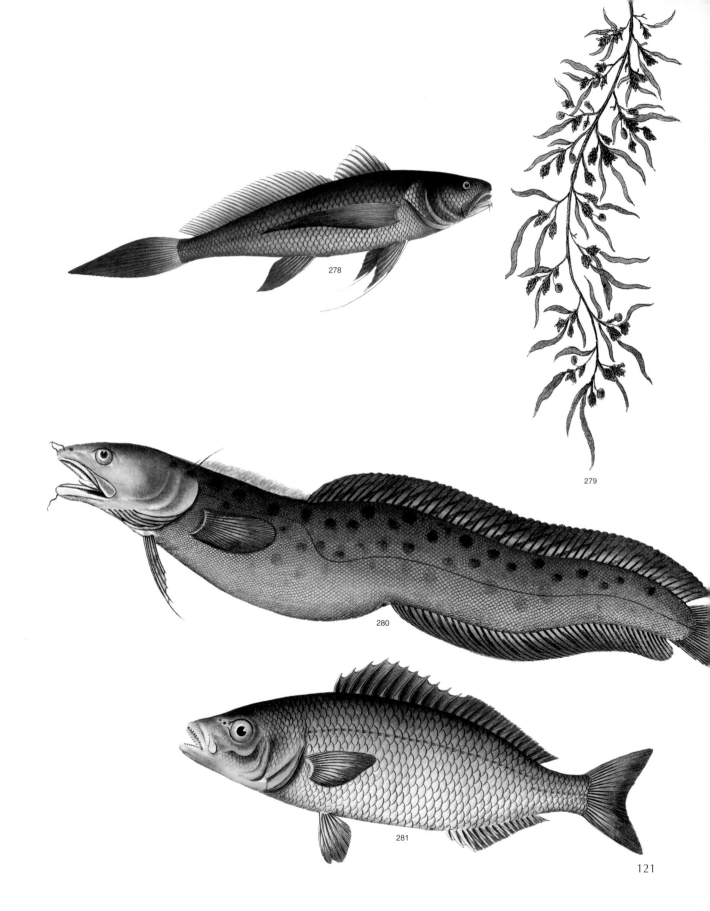

278

279

280

281

282

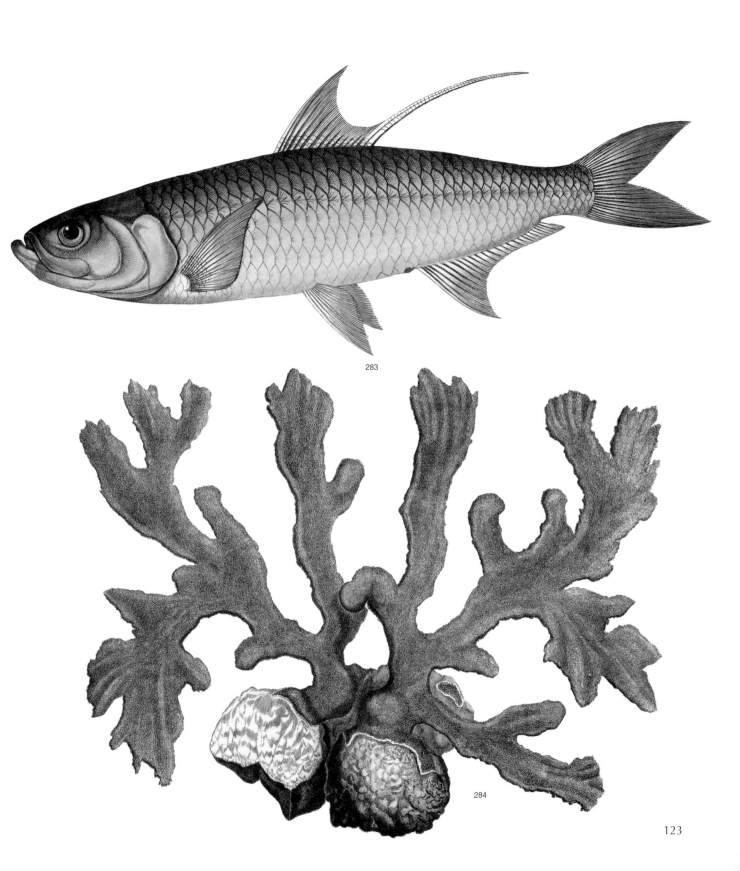

283

284

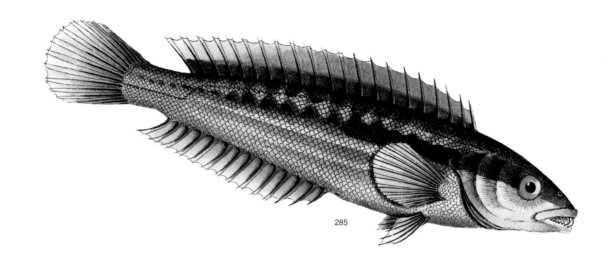

285

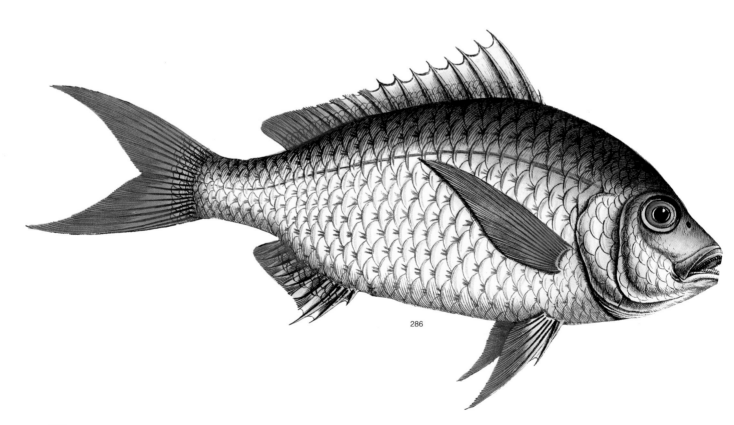

286

287

288

289

290

291

292

293

294